THE BOOK OF TOASTY'S

WRITTEN & ILLUSTRATED BY NiCKY HANLEY

Published by Toasty Publications.

For encouragement, ideas and helping me along the way:

Thank you to Mum, Dad and all my family.

Thank you to Peggy and Evie.

Thank you to Elephants Class 2024.

And thank you for reading this book!

Copyright© 2024 by Nicky Hanley.

All rights reserved.

No part of this publication may be reproduced, distributed, or transmitted in any form or by any means, including photocopying, recording, or other electronic or mechanical methods, without the prior written permission of the publisher, except as permitted by U.K. copyright law.

Book Cover Design by Nicky Hanley.

Illustrations by Nicky Hanley.

First edition 2024.

ISBN: 9798883796721

*For anyone who's had a dream
(they can come true!)*

#1 TOASTY

#2 KING TOASTY

#3 Fire Toasty

#4 COOL TOASTY

#5 ZOMBIE TOASTY

#6 Wormhole Toasty

#7 EVIL TOASTY

#8 GHOSTY TOASTY

#9 SUPER TOASTY

#10 BOXER TOASTY

#11 CUP TOASTY

#12 TOESTY

#13 SHORTS TOASTY

#14 CAT TOASTY

#15 PHONE TOASTY

#16 PASTA TOASTY

#17 HOT TOASTY

#18 CRISP TOASTY

#19 CHEESE TOASTY

#20 DEAD TOASTY

#21 TRAIN TOASTY

#23 DRAGON TOASTY

#24 JAM TOASTY

#25 ROBO TOASTY

#27 CHRISTMAS TOASTY

#28 TOAST-NADO

#29 PANDA TOASTY

#30 Bird Toasty

#31 OUTLET TOASTY

#32 KNIGHT TOASTY

#33 Fireman Toasty

#34 GRIM REAPER TOASTY

#35 WOODEN TOASTY

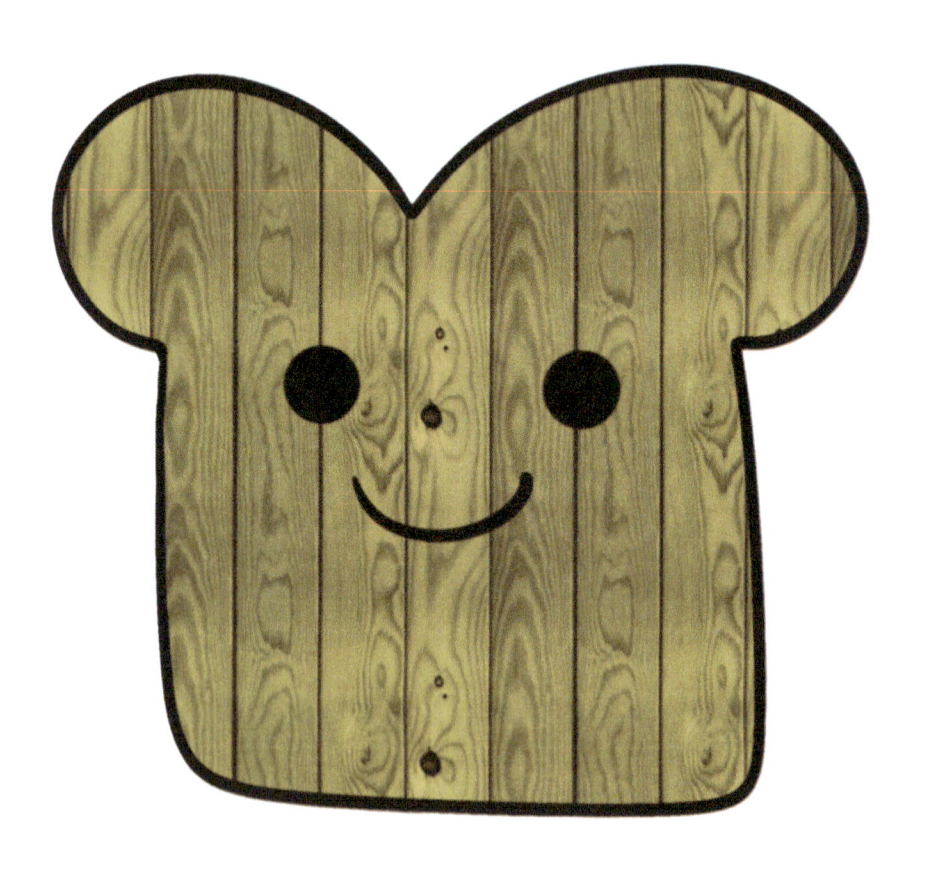

#36 BUILDER TOASTY

#37 SHOCKED TOASTY

#38 WATERMELON TOASTY

#39 GAMER TOASTY

#40 INFINITY TOASTY

#41 ELEPHANT TOASTY

#42 TOASTER TOASTY

#43 KARATE TOASTY

#44 BURNT TOASTY

#45 BOOK TOASTY

once upon a time there was a Toasty

The end

#46 COAT TOASTY

#47 BABY TOASTY

GOO GOO

#48 GRANDAD TOASTY

#49 DEMONIC TOASTY

#50 RAPUNZEL TOASTY

#51 FISH TOASTY

#52 ROCKET TOASTY

#53 BIGFOOT TOASTY

#54 RICH TOASTY

#55 BASKETBALL TOASTY

#56 COWBOY TOASTY

"YEE HA!"

#57 Pirate Toasty

#58 UNI-TOASTY

#59 CLOCK TOASTY

#60 ASTRO TOASTY

#62 TEACHER TOASTY

1+1=2
2+2=4

#63 CAMP TOASTY

#64 FAIRY TOASTY

#65 TEA AND TOASTY

#66 RELAXED TOASTY

#67 DETECTIVE TOASTY

#68 ALIEN TOASTY

#69 PIG TOASTY

#70 NINJA TOASTY

#71 BAGUETTEY

#72 DONUT TOASTY

#73 RACECAR TOASTY

VROOM

#74 PINEAPPLE TOASTY

#75 OCTO-TOASTY

#76 BIG TOASTY

#77 REINDEER TOASTY

#78 SANTA TOASTY

#79 MUM TOASTY

#80 HAT TOASTY

#81 REALISTIC TOASTY

#82 MATHS TOASTY

#83 CHEF TOASTY

#84 WAFFLE TOASTY

#85 CACTUS TOASTY

#86 SURFIN' TOASTY

#87 CUPCAKE TOASTY

#88 ART TOASTY

#89 Eiffel Tower Toasty

#90 BUFF TOASTY

#91 BOBA TOASTY

#92 EGG TOASTY

#93 CHOCOLATE TOASTY

CHOCOLATE

#94 FURRY TOASTY

#95 TOILET TOASTY

#96 SKATER TOASTY

#97 iNViSiBLE TOASTY

#98 TALL TOASTY

#99 MERMAID TOASTY

#100 Final Toasty

"THE END!"

DRAW YOUR OWN TOASTY

crazy hair

101

102

301

#104 BoB Toasty

Printed in Great Britain
by Amazon